T0198981

Bola Jones

Baby Steps with Christ

A Quick Easy Step by Step Guide to Knowing Jesus Everyday

AuthorHouse™ UK
1663 Liberty Drive
Bloomington, IN 47403 USA
www.authorhouse.co.uk
UK TFN: 0800 0148641 (Toll Free inside the UK)
UK Local: 02036 956322 (+44 20 3695 6322 from outside the UK)

This book is printed on acid-free paper.

ISBN: 978-1-6655-8986-4 (sc)
978-1-6655-8985-7 (e)

Print information available on the last page.

Published by AuthorHouse 07/30/2021

authorHOUSE®

Acknowledgement

This book was birth in my heart a few years ago. It only became a reality during the 2020 pandemic while under lockdown in London. I am grateful that God used such a trying time that touched the whole world to produce a message so simple. The COVID-19 pandemic has been a profound reminder that no matter who we are or where we are located, our time on earth is limited and can come to an end at any given moment. Baby steps with Christ is for all who seek to journey with God here on earth and be prepared for a joyful reunion with Him at the end of that journey. My deep gratitude to Michael Christisking who laboured with me in the summer of 2019 in Houston, Texas to develop the outline of this book. Further gratitude to his daughter, Rejoice Christisking who during our shared summer spent in lockdown in London, England, diligently edited this book.

Number 1

What just happened to me?

When you invite Jesus Christ into your heart, you are created anew. Your spirit is reborn through the Holy Spirit which is the Spirit of God Himself. The Bible calls this being born again. You are now a child of God and a member of His family.

Jesus Christ is the first and only person in the Bible to declare that without being born again, no one can go to heaven:

"Truly, truly, I say to you, unless one is born again he cannot see the kingdom of God"

John 3:3 (ESV)

Jesus made it clear that this was very different from our physical birth which comes through our earthly parents. Spiritual rebirth can only happen when the Spirit of God comes into our hearts. He will only come into our heart if we invite Jesus in to become our Lord and Saviour. So, if you have just done that, congratulations! You have been born again! You are a new creation!

Number 2

Saying goodbye to My old life

"Therefore, if anyone is in Christ, he is a new creation; old things have passed away; behold, all things have become new."

2 Cor 5:17 (NKJV)

Now that you are a new creation there are active steps you will need to take for the life of Christ deposited in you to be fully lived out.

A decision to follow Christ will mean nothing if there is no intention to leave your old way of living behind. This is why it is important that you start to learn what the bible says about how to live for Christ.

As you learn to read and live by the bible, you may find that some things you used to do, places you used to go or people you choose to spend time with are not compatible with the new life God is calling you to.

As you make up your mind to wholly follow Jesus, you will be empowered by the Holy Spirit to walk away from aspects of your old life that do not line up with your new life in Christ.

Beginning a new life

Becoming a participating member of a community of Christians who actively follow Christ will be essential for the journey ahead. Find a church with bible-based teaching, preaching and prayer. This will provide the foundation you will need to grow and develop in your new walk with Jesus. As a Christian, you now belong to the family of God. You are a member of His body which is the church. Christ is the head of His church. Every part of the body has a role to play and need to be connected to each other and the head which is Christ in order to function properly. So, get connected into a body of believers who are connected to Jesus Christ. You will soon find yourself growing day by day with an increasing love for Jesus and an understanding of your new identity in Him

"And He put all things under His feet, and gave Him to be head over all things to the church, which is His body, the fullness of Him who fills all in all."

Ephesians 1:22-23 (NKJV)

Speaking differently

"A good man out of the good treasure of his heart brings forth good; and an evil man out of the evil treasure of his heart brings forth evil. For out of the abundance of the heart his mouth speaks."

Luke 6:45(NKJV)

As we spend more and more time with Jesus, the Holy Spirit changes the condition of our heart. As our heart changes, all other things we do also change. This should become evident in the way we speak. Our words have a life of their own and can create something good or cause incredible pain and destruction. With the Holy Spirit now living inside of you, you are empowered to choose the words that you speak so that they are glorifying to God and build others up, not tear them down. We become more aware of how destructive gossip is and dishonouring to God and people. We learn to refrain from criticizing others or worse, backbiting. With the help of the Holy Spirit and our willingness to obey God, we will increase in our ability for self-control including how we react and respond to others with our words.

Thinking differently

For as a man thinketh, so is he

Prov 23:7 (KJV)

And do not be conformed to this world, but be transformed by the renewing of your mind, that you may prove what is that good and acceptable and perfect will of God.

Roman's 12:2 NKJV

It is impossible to live for God without knowing the mind of God. God has enabled us to know His mind through the Holy Spirit who is deposited in us when we invite Jesus Christ into our heart. Learning to know, understand and follow God requires us to continually renew our mind. As we spend time in the bible, prayer and fellowship with other Christians, our minds become transformed by the Spirit of God. This transformation allows us to know what Gods will is for us in every situation we face. Sometimes we still get things wrong, but God uses even our mistakes and errors to conform us to His will for our lives. Through our mistakes, we learn to understand the unique way God chooses to communicate and guide each and every one of His children.

Living differently

As you learn to live the new life which is Christ in you, just like a baby you start with little steps. You will experience slips and falls but it will be worth the experience of learning how your heavenly Father cares for you. You will come to know more and more of God's love for you and this will start to create new desires in your heart. The desire to know God more, to obey Him, to fellowship with the rest of Gods family which is the church and to reach out to others with God's love. The closer you draw to God; the more Christ becomes the center of your life. The more Christ-centered you become, the more you will be able to impact other people's lives with God's blessings.

I have been crucified with Christ; it is no longer I who live, but Christ lives in me; and the life which I now live in the flesh I live by faith in the Son of God, who loved me and gave Himself for me

Galatians 2:20 (NKJV)

Number Three

What it means to be in Christ

Trusting Christ

The life of the Christian is one of trust and obedience. This is a decision that we need to make for ourselves. As you grow in your relationship with Jesus, you will come to find He is exactly who He says He is and He is faithful to His word. The journey of the Christian life will take you through many experiences that will demonstrate God's love and unwavering commitment to you. While friends and sometimes even family may fail you, Jesus will always be with you. You will find He is with you in your worst of times as well as your best of times. It is this experience that helps to build the trust that you will need for a lifetime of walking with Jesus.

For I am convinced that neither death nor life, neither angels nor demons, neither the present nor the future, nor any powers, neither height nor depth, nor anything else in all creation, will be able to separate us from the love of God that is in Christ Jesus our Lord.

Romans 8:38-39 (NIV)

Obeying Christ

Obedience to the word of God is a choice that we will need to make on a daily basis. The more we choose to obey God, the more evident will be His power at work in our lives. Obedience can sometimes seem to have a high price tag but always proves to be worth it in the end. God does and will not force anyone to do as He says. He has given each individual free will to choose. The choices we make however have consequences.

See, I set before you today life and prosperity, death and destruction. For I command you today to love the Lord your God, to walk in obedience to him, and to keep his commands, decrees and laws; then you will live and increase, and the Lord your God will bless you in the land you are entering to possess.

Deuteronomy 30: 15-16 (NIV)

Sharing Christ

Consequently, faith comes from hearing the message, and the message is heard through the word about Christ

Romans 10:17 (NIV)

You have been given new life through the word of God. Like most people, that word came to you through someone else. When you heard the word about salvation through Jesus Christ, it produced faith in your heart and you chose to receive the invitation of Christ to you to follow Him.

There are many others around you who need to know about this invitation from Christ for eternal life. Share what God has done in your heart with others. Let them know that the gift of salvation and eternal life are freely available to them if they will choose to receive it as you have done.

Number Four

Your new life is a walk

Now you have given your life to Christ, you are born again. Like a newborn baby, you will be learning to walk with Christ. You will feel weak and unsteady at times and may have times when you slip, slide, and even fall, but this is all a part of your learning process. You will need the company of other believers and good teaching on walking with Christ. If you are wise you will hold yourself accountable to others. This is a very beautiful part of your journey with Christ as you learn your new identity in Him and grow in confidence of who God has created you to be and His incredible plan for your unique life.

"but they that wait upon the Lord shall renew their strength; they shall mount up with wings as eagles, they shall run and not be weary, and they shall walk and not faint."

Isaiah 40:31 (KJV)

A Race

Your new journey is also a race in many ways. It is a race against time as your present life on earth will come to an end. It is a race because there is a finish line for every believer. It is also a race because there is a crown promised for those who endure until the end. An athlete trains to win by keeping themselves in shape, watching what they eat, ensuring they get adequate rest and training themselves in speed and endurance. Likewise, the Christian race requires we stay in shape spiritually, eat well by feeding on the word of God while staying away from unhealthy habits that will contaminate our spiritual lives, train ourselves in spiritual disciplines which bring speed and endurance such as praying and fasting, and taking the time to rest.

Everyone who competes in the games goes into strict training. They do it to get a crown that will not last, but we do it to get a crown that will last forever.

I Corinthians 9:25 (NIV)

Similarly, anyone who competes as an athlete does not receive the victor's crown except by competing according to the rules.

2 Timothy 2:5 (NIV)

A Fight

When you chose to follow Christ, you crossed over from darkness into light. This is not just a metaphor. These two states of being represent two kingdoms which are at war.

For we wrestle not against flesh and blood, but against principalities, against powers, against the rulers of the darkness of this world, against spiritual wickedness in high places.

Ephesians 6:12-13 (KJV)

But we can be confident in Jesus Christ who has gone before us to show us the way.

And the light shineth in darkness; and the darkness comprehended it not.

John 1:5 (KJV)

A Journey

Your new life in Christ is also a journey which starts here on earth and stretches into eternity where you will get to live in God's presence forever. It is impossible to take this journey on earth without using the map which God has provided which is the Holy Bible. The bible provides all the directions, signposts, and encouragement you will need for every step of the journey. There are times during the journey when you may feel weary, doubtful, anxious, or even fearful. The word of God which is contained in the Bible is actually the power of God. So, as you read it, you will receive power to overcome whatever difficulty you encounter along the way. When you read and share it with others, you will encounter even more of God's power.

For the word of God is living and active and sharper than any two-edged sword and piercing as far as the division of soul and spirit, of both joints and marrow, and able to judge the thoughts and intentions of the heart.

Hebrews 4:12 (NASB)

NUMBER FIVE

WHO IS ON YOUR TEAM

Knowing the father

Our earthly fathers are meant to be a picture of our heavenly father but in many cases may not be and in some quite the opposite. Whether we have an earthly father who lived up to this call or not, we are assured of a heavenly father. God the father longs for us to not only know Him but to be in active relationship with him. When you said yes to Jesus, the Holy Spirit starts to bear witness within you that you are a child of God. You come to know God as Father.

The Spirit you received does not make you slaves, so that you live in fear again; rather, the Spirit you received brought about your adoption to sonship. And by him we cry, "Abba, Father."

Romans 8:15 (NIV)

Knowing the Son

We cannot see God because He is Spirit. God expressed Himself in human flesh through Jesus Christ whom the bible refers to as God's only begotten son. Jesus was born of the Holy Spirit and is both fully man and fully God. Jesus enables us to see God and in knowing Jesus, we come to know God.

The Son is the radiance of God's glory and the exact representation of his being.

Hebrews 1:3a (NIV)

Jesus came to take the place of Adam, the first man through whom sin entered into the human race. Jesus went to the cross to bear the punishment that was due to Adam and all of humanity. When we put our trust in Jesus, He takes away our sin and gives us His righteousness in exchange.

For He made Him who knew no sin to be sin for us, that we might become the righteousness of God in Him.

2 Corinthians 5:21 (NKJV)

Knowing the Holy Spirit

The Holy Spirit enables us to hear God speak and also helps us to pray. The Holy Spirit also serves as our comforter and guide. He brings the Bible alive in our hearts as we read and meditate on its words. We can grieve the Holy Spirit with our words, thoughts, and actions.

And grieve not the holy Spirit of God, whereby ye are sealed unto the day of redemption. Let all bitterness, and wrath, and anger, and clamor, and evil speaking, be put away from you, with all malice: And be ye kind one to another, tenderhearted, forgiving one another, even as God for Christ's sake hath forgiven you.

Ephesians 4:30-32

But the fruit of the Spirit is love, joy, peace, longsuffering, kindness, goodness, faithfulness,] gentleness, self-control. Against such there is no law.

Galatians 5:22-23

Knowing the people of God

The people of God are His family. The family of God are made up of brothers and sisters who are all learning to relate to God as their heavenly Father. Each and every one of God's children has a special place in His family including you. It is important that you take your place in God's family and learn to walk with your brothers and sisters in unity and in love. Like every human relationship, there will be times of testing and disappointment and there may even be one or two hurtful experiences. We will need to learn to forgive and show mercy to each other. It is these relationships that will enable us to grow as children of God and cause others to recognize God in us by the love we have for each other.

By this shall all men know that ye are my disciples, if ye have love one for another.

John 13:35 (KJV)

Chapter Six

WHO ARE YOUR OPPONENTS?

Knowing Satan

Satan was once an angel in heaven until he led a rebellion against God. Satan and the angels who followed him in his rebellion against God have since been cast out of heaven and have only a very limited time left before they face destruction in hell. Until that time, Satan is determined to take as many people to hell with him as possible and to make life intolerable on earth especially for those who choose to follow Christ. When you decided to follow Jesus, you not only entered into the victory which Jesus won on the Cross over sin and death, but over Satan as well. Nevertheless, as a child of God, Satan will still try to bombard you with lies, trials and temptations.

Therefore, rejoice, O heavens and you who dwell in them! But woe to you, O earth and sea, for the devil has come down to you in great wrath, because he knows that his time in short!

Rev 12:12 (ESV)

Be alert and of sober mind. Your enemy the devil, prowls around like a roaring lion looking for someone to devour.

1 Peter 5:8

Knowing the world

As a believer in Christ, you will soon find that your new life is at odds with many of those who do not follow Christ . Your daily challenge will be not to conform to the world around you, but to be daily transformed into who God has created you to be.

Do not be conformed to this world, but be transformed by the renewal of your mind, that by testing you may discern what is the will of God, what is good and acceptable and perfect." ... Then you will learn to know God's will for you, which is good and pleasing and perfect."

Romans 12:2 (ESV)

Knowing the flesh

When you invited Jesus into your heart, the Holy Spirit took up residence in your spirit. Your flesh however is already under the condemnation of sin and opposes the things of the Spirit. So do not be surprised that you will still have to exercise the authority of the Holy Spirit over the temptations of your flesh as you choose to daily walk with Christ

"But I say, walk by the Spirit, and you will not gratify the desires of the flesh." For the desires of the flesh are against the Spirit, and the desires of the Spirit are against the flesh, for these are opposed to each other, to keep you from doing the things you want to do.

Galatians 5:16-17 ESV

The acts of the flesh are obvious: sexual immorality, impurity and debauchery; idolatry and witchcraft; hatred, discord, jealousy, fits of rage, selfish ambition, dissensions, factions and envy; drunkenness, orgies, and the like. I warn you, as I did before, that those who live like this will not inherit the kingdom of God.

Galatians 5:19-21 (NIV)

Knowing the double minded

You will encounter people along your journey both inside and outside the church who are double-minded. They have one foot in the world and the other in the things of God. They talk the talk but do not necessarily walk the walk. You will need to be vigilante so that you do not find yourself being led astray by those who are not fully committed to following Jesus.

Do not merely listen to the word, and so deceive yourselves. Do what it says. Anyone who listens to the word but does not do what it says is like someone who looks at his face in a mirror and, after looking at himself, goes away and immediately forgets what he looks like. But whoever looks intently into the perfect law that gives freedom, and continues in it—not forgetting what they have heard, but doing it—they will be blessed in what they do.

James 1:22-25 (NIV)

Chapter Seven

Standing firm in Christ

As you walk with Jesus, you will learn to use various tools that God has provided to enable you to stand firm in Christ. This includes walking in truth, trusting in the righteousness and salvation provided by faith in Jesus, living in peace with others, learning and being ready to share the word of God whenever you have the opportunity.

Therefore, take up the whole armor of God, that you may be able to withstand in the evil day, and having done all, to stand firm. Stand therefore, having fastened on the belt of truth, and having put on the breastplate of righteousness, and, as shoes for your feet, having put on the readiness given by the gospel of peace. In all circumstances take up the shield of faith, with which you can extinguish all the flaming darts of the evil one; and take the helmet of salvation, and the sword of the Spirit, which is the word of God.

Ephesians 6:13-17 (ESV)

Knowing who you are in Christ

Your new identity in Christ will be central to your walk with Him. God wants you to be confident in your Christ-given identity. The world and Satan will fight hard to make you assume an identity different from that which God has given you. The aim of the world is to make you conform. God's intention is to transform you into who He created you to be.

For freedom Christ has set us free; stand firm therefore, and do not submit again to a yoke of slavery.

Galatians 5:1 (ESV)

Do not be conformed to this world, but be transformed by the renewal of your mind, that by testing you may discern what is the will of God, what is good and acceptable and perfect." ... Then you will learn to know God's will for you, which is good and pleasing and perfect."

Romans 12:2 (ESV)

Learning to Resist temptation

As a Christian, you will still face temptation but with the power of the Holy Spirit now living in you, you have the weapon you need to overcome. It will take consistent use and practice to learn to resist and overcome the many temptations the devil will bring your way. The more you put your weapons to use, the less power the devil will be able to muster against you

Submit yourselves therefore to God. Resist the devil, and he will flee from you.

James 4:7 (ESV)

Learning how to Walk by faith

Walking with God is an act of faith. It is by faith that we believe God created all the things we can see. It is also by faith that we believe He will bring to pass things that we do not yet see. God delights in and rewards your faith even if it is as tiny as a mustard seed. Jesus promises that your faith can move mountains. As you learn to seek God and bring your petitions before Him, you will soon start to experience answers to prayer which will further encourage your faith.

Now faith is the assurance of things hoped for, the conviction of things not seen

Hebrews 11:1 (ESV)

And without faith it is impossible to please him, for whoever would draw near to God must believe that he exists and that he rewards those who seek him.

Hebrews 11:6 (ESV)

Learning how to pray

Prayer takes discipline. The Holy Spirit helps us to pray according to God's will. Jesus is also constantly praying for us. While on earth, Jesus taught His disciples the following approach to prayer

Pray then like this: "Our Father in heaven,
hallowed be your name. Your kingdom
come, your will be done,
on earth as it is in heaven. Give us this day our
daily bread, and forgive us our debts,
as we also have forgiven our debtors. And lead us
not into temptation but deliver us from evil.

Mathew 6:9-13

Learning how to Live in the word of God.

The word of God is to your spirit, what food is to your body. If you go without eating you will gradually waste away and if prolonged, you will die. Likewise, if you do not feed your spirit with the word of God regularly, your spirit will become malnourished and lose its connection to Jesus and eventually die.

Learning how to Maintain fellowship with God's people

It is important to stay connected to other Christians. Also keep in mind that other Christians like yourself are on a journey. This means no one is perfect. So as with other relationships, we will need to learn to relate and get along with our brothers and sisters in Christ. This will include learning to forgive and even overlook offenses. We will not be made perfect until we all see Christ again face to face.

Not neglecting to meet together, as is the habit of some, but encouraging one another, and all the more as you see the Day drawing near.

Hebrews 10:25

Learning how to Share your testimony

The story of how you met Jesus is your testimony. It is a story that will be a powerful tool throughout your life as a Christian. Every time you share it, you make God real to others. It is also a good reminder for you of how much God loves you and what He did to get your attention. Sharing Your testimony also serves to protect you spiritually against the attacks of the enemy

And they have conquered him by the blood of the Lamb and by the word of their testimony,...

Revelation 12:11 (ESV)

Learning to Give

God is very generous and wants to reflect that part of Him through us. As a new Christian, God will start to train you on how to share the blessings He gives you with others including your time, attention, care, finances, and other gifts to those in need around you. One of the most effective ways to cultivate giving is through the paying of your tithes to your local church which represents 10% of your earnings. As you learn to be faithful in this small thing, you will find God trusting you with increasing responsibility to share with others. You will also find that God is more than faithful to meet your needs.

Give, and it will be given to you. Good measure, pressed down, shaken together, running over, will be put into your lap. For with the measure you use it will be measured back to you."

Luke 6:38 (ESV)

Learning to Forgive

We are commanded by God to forgive others. Offenses are going to happen both within and outside the church. The reason why Jesus went to the Cross was so that we could be forgiven our sins. If we choose not to forgive other, this makes it impossible to receive God's forgiveness. Forgiving those who offend, wound, or hurt us is for our own good not theirs.

But if you do not forgive others, then your Father will not forgive your transgressions.

Mathew 6:15 (NASB)

Chapter Eight

The necessity of Baptism with the Holy Spirit

But the Helper, the Holy Spirit, whom the Father will send in my name, he will teach you all things and bring to your remembrance all that I have said to you.

John 14:26 (ESV)

Jesus promised the Holy Spirit will help us in our journey through life as a Christian. The Holy Spirit is the Spirit of God. He speaks to us through the Word of God, He prays alongside us and He puts Gods direction for us in our minds and helps us to understand it. We experience the baptism of the Holy Spirit by asking For His indwelling through prayer.

The Necessity of Baptism with Water

When all the people were being baptized, Jesus was baptized too. And as he was praying, heaven was opened

Luke 3:21 (NIV)

Having been buried with him in baptism, in which you were also raised with him through your faith in the working of God, who raised him from the dead.

Colossians 2:12(NIV)

Jesus set us an example by getting baptized Himself even though He was God in human flesh. He commanded that everyone who chooses to follow Him should get baptized by the water and the Holy Spirit. This represents the laying down of the old life and the putting on of a new life.

The necessity of Holy communion

Holy Communion is an act of remembrance, remembering the death of Christ on the Cross. Jesus Himself took communion with His disciples at what is famously referred to as the Last supper. He did this with what He referred to as the bread and the cup to demonstrate the breaking of His body and the shedding of His blood on the cross. He then commanded His disciples to continue to do this in remembrance of Him. Today, Christians all over the world come together in their various churches to take communion together.

And when He had given thanks, He broke it and said, "This is My body, which is for you; do this in remembrance of Me. In the same way He took the cup also after supper, saying, "This cup is the new covenant in My blood; do this, as often as you drink it, in remembrance of Me."

1 Corinthians 11:24-25 (NASB)

The necessity of serving

One of the best ways for growing your faith in Christ is through service. There are many opportunities to do this in church and through church to your local community and the world beyond. As you start to reach out to others with the love of Christ, you will find your faith getting stronger and the love of God being poured in ever increasing measure into your heart and out to others.

So also, faith by itself if it does not have works, is dead.

James 2:17 (ESV)

The necessity of accountability

It is important to not walk alone. You will need the help of others as you learn to walk with Jesus. It helps to spend time in fellowship with other Christians and also develop a relationship with a trusted person who you can share your struggles with openly.

As iron sharpens iron, so one person sharpens another.

Proverbs 27:17 (NIV)

Therefore, confess your sins to one another, and pray for one another so that you may be healed. A prayer of a righteous person, when it is brought about, can accomplish much.

James 5:16 (NASB)

Chapter Nine

Winning souls and making disciples

One of the greatest joys of becoming a Christian is getting to share the good news of the gospel with others. You will experience so much of God's amazing love and the peace that comes with forgiveness that you would want the same for your loved ones. When you experience God touch others through your life, it will encourage you to continue to reach out. As you grow in your faith, you will learn how to help others follow Jesus. This is called discipling.

The fruit of the righteous is a tree of life,
And he who is wise wins souls.

Proverbs 11:30 (NASB)

Love is your life

The mark of the true Christian is love. Love for God and love for others. As you walk with Christ, the evidence of your growth will be displayed in your willingness to forgive those who hurt or offend you, reach out to those in need around you and share the love of Christ with others.

"And you shall love the Lord your God with all your heart and with all your soul and with all your mind and with all your strength. The second is this: 'You shall love your neighbor as yourself.' There is no other commandment greater than these."

Mark 12:30-31 (ESV)

Faith is your master key

Throughout your journey as a Christian, you will experience moments where what you believe about God will be tested. You may face situations that seem impossible or an experience that seems unfair, even unjust. In these difficult moments you will need to keep going back to the word of God to remind yourself what is true. As you hold onto God's word by faith, you will experience victory in and through every test or trial that will prove God's faithfulness to you.

Now faith is the assurance of things hoped for, the conviction of things not seen.

Hebrews 11:1 (ESV)

Holiness is your lifestyle

A tree is known by the fruit that it produces. Likewise, a true Christian will have a lifestyle that is in line with what the bible says. As you walk in obedience to Christ, His Spirit in you will help you let go of ways and thought patterns, attitudes and behaviors that are not in keeping with the word of God. The fruit of the Spirit will also start to become more and more evident in you as you chose to walk with Christ every day.

But the fruit of the Spirit is love, joy, peace, patience, kindness, goodness, faithfulness,

Galatians 5:22 (NASB)

Blessed is your life in every way

When you chose to follow Jesus, you handed over your life into His care. This means that He watches over you continually and prays for you without ceasing. He is your defender, provider and will direct your steps if you choose to seek Him daily. You are not guaranteed freedom from difficulty or hardship and your faith may even mean that you will face certain struggles. However, God promises your life can never be taken out of His hand and He will work all things together for your good.

But blessed are those who trust in the LORD and have made the LORD their hope and confidence.

Jer 17:7 (NLT)

And we know that for those who love God all things work together for good, for those who are called according to his purpose.

Romans 8:28 (ESV)

Chapter Ten

Heaven is your home

One day, your time on earth will come to an end. Your choice to follow Jesus and live your life in obedience to Him and His word guarantees that you will spend eternity with Him in heaven. Heaven is a place that is beyond our best imagination and wildest dreams. It is a place where we have been guaranteed eternal rest and peace in the presence of God Himself and in fellowship with all of our brothers and sisters from every part of the earth.

And if I go and prepare a place for you, I will come again and will take you to myself, that where I am you may be also.

John 14:3 (ESV)

And He will wipe away every tear from their eyes; and there will no longer be any death; there will no longer be any mourning, or crying, or pain; the first things have passed away."

Revelation 21:4 (NASB)

Conclusion

Once again, welcome to the family of God and to a lifelong journey that will lead to eternity in heaven.

If you have not yet made a decision to follow Christ, you can do so this very moment by praying the following simple prayer:

Dear Jesus,

Thank you for dying for me on the Cross. I repent of my sins and ask for your forgiveness. I invite you to come into my heart as my Lord and saviour. I surrender my life into your loving hands and ask you to help me to follow you the rest of my days. Thank you for saving me. Amen.

Printed in the United States
by Baker & Taylor Publisher Services